THE EASTER PEOPLE

A BACKWARD GLANCE AT THE OLD CHURCH SHOWS THE WEATHER-VANE ARROW AND GLITTERING BALL AND THE STEADFAST CLOCK FACE BENEATH

The Easter People

A Pen-picture
of the
Moravian Celebration
of the
Resurrection

✛

By
Winifred Kirkland
Author of *Polly Pal's Parish*, **etc.**

HERITAGE BOOKS
2008

HERITAGE BOOKS

AN IMPRINT OF HERITAGE BOOKS, INC.

Books, CDs, and more—Worldwide

For our listing of thousands of titles see our website
at
www.HeritageBooks.com

A Facsimile Reprint
Published 2008 by
HERITAGE BOOKS, INC.
Publishing Division
100 Railroad Ave. #104
Westminster, Maryland 21157

International Standard Book Numbers
Paperbound: 978-1-58549-980-9
Clothbound: 978-0-7884-7574-0

FOREWORD

A NYONE who has ever been an eye-witness of the beautiful Easter customs which these pages commemorate must feel how inadequate is any description of a Salem Easter. This account, in a form shortened for magazine requirements, appeared in *The Ladies' Home Journal* of April, 1922, and it is with the kind permission of the editors that narrative and illustrations are here reprinted.

W. K.

Asheville, N. C.

CONTENTS

THE OLD HOME CHURCH WITH ITS
UNFAILING CLOCK FACE IN
THE GABLE BENEATH
THE BELFRY

I

OLD SALEM TODAY

THE approach to old Salem of the old South is commonplace enough. Thirty miles of motoring roll away beneath our wheels. Prosperous fields to right and left spread to woody reaches that circle the horizon. The hesitant leaves of an early spring blur the stark outlines of trunk and branch. Gnarled orchard boughs are all in milk-white flower. Against dusky wood spaces the Judas tree hangs its veils of deep pink, and the dogwood is just beginning to show the glint of silver disks. Other cars go honking past us. On the railroad parallel to us a train thunders by. We mount a hill and the twin city of Winston-Salem lies before us. We dip down the slope, then climb again, and abruptly we are in another world, we are in old Salem. I shall never again forget that the word Salem means peace.

After two heavy, gray days, the sun, at

noon of Good Friday, comes riding forth clear of all cloud. The boxwood in old gardens is crisp and glistening. House walls of ancient brick, freshened by the rain, yield their full of mellow colour. As we roll up South Main Street, my companion points out this and that place of interest, for she is one of the many far-scattered Southern women who once were schoolgirls in the old Moravian Female Academy. The word Moravian has up to this time been merely a word to me, a term associated with quaint, long-persistent customs, but in a few brief days that word is to become potent with a significance that I feel inadequate to express, as hesitatingly and gratefully I try to set down the impressions of one chance visitor. In every recurrent springtime thousands and thousands of such visitors push into the old city, and at every Easter-tide by some strange contagion of reverence, quiet Salem has the power to subdue these alien crowds to the very spirit of its own piety. Such is the alchemy of influence possessed by the people who have made Easter the pivot of all the year, the very heart of all their faith and all their conduct.

Almost at once as we enter the town I am aware of an atmosphere vibrant with expectancy.   Windows are being polished, and dooryards clipped, and faces lifted to us brighten with unspoken welcome.   Old houses abut directly on the pavement, so that their modern occupants must have thick curtains for privacy, curtains now snowy starched for Easter. Some of the roomy dwellings have nestling beside them the little shops where once the master kept his business close to home.   Externally most of the houses remain exactly as they were when first built, in the later eighteenth century.   We pass the old Butner Tavern, standing just as it stood in 1781 when Washington occupied that now famous northeast chamber.   In the museum there is still exhibited the harpsichord by which he was entertained, and the story runs that a little girl selected to play, broke down, and was kissed and comforted by the great first president himself.

We turn to our right at the time-worn Square, a stretching rectangle of towering water oaks crossed by diagonal paths.   At opposite sides of the corner at which we enter are buildings that recall the deep community fellowship characteristic of the Moravian practice, for one of the two is the Widows' House, and the other, with its red-tiled roof and deep windows, is the House of the Single Brothers, where, for many years, before it became the present museum, they had their school for boys. We are facing now the long, unbroken brick façade that forms the entire east side of the Square. In the middle is the Academy, with its high white pillars, and at the south the Sisters' House with its two rows of dormer windows. At the north stands the old Home Church, with its staunch ancient walls dull red beneath bright ivy, its hooded door, its unfailing clock face in the gable beneath the domed white belfry. At the church we turn northward and get out of our car to search for the little cottage where we are to have rooms. Our motor cannot go farther, for all cars are barred from the long quiet avenue that lies before us. My friend is looking sadly for the great shaggy trees familiar to her girlhood, those towering ancient guardians of the dead that gave Cedar Avenue its name.

WITHIN THESE PORTALS STRETCHES ROW AFTER
ROW OF LITTLE, FLAT, WHITE GRAVESTONES

But now those old trees themselves are dead, and their place taken by slim young poplars freshly green with spring. To me, the newcomer, Cedar Avenue is beautiful enough as it is today, a broad white gravelled path lined by the swaying green shafts of the poplars, and bordered on our left by a low stone wall, and on the right by a high picket fence, almost covered by ivy, and broken by white-arched gateways, on which, above the green-leaved pillars, are blazoned triumphant Easter texts. Within those portals in sunshine that is dappled by the shadows of cedar and boxwood stretches row after row of little flat white gravestones all exactly alike. Here is no distinction of persons nor of families, but merely of groups, married men together, married women, single men and boys and boy babies, single women and girls and girl babies. This green spot is the center of Salem; it is the center of the Moravian faith. This is the graveyard where, near and dear and instant in the memory of the living, the dead lie, asleep in sunny peace.

Nestling close to the graves is the little cottage, cheery with nodding tulips and bright hyacinths, where we are to stay with Miss Dorcas Reitzer, and her niece, Miss Bertha. Both are of old Moravian stock, readily tracing all their ancestors back to German Herrnhut of 1722. Miss Dorcas is eighty, her feet are slow with rheumatism, but her mind and heart are alert for one more exultant Easter. Along the gravel path beyond her door people are constantly passing on their way to the green and white graveyard, for the houses of the dead as well as the houses of the living must be shining clean and flower-trimmed for Easter morning.

II

GOOD FRIDAY IN SALEM

THERE is but one way to know any creed, and that is by knowing the people who have lived it. It is because of the welcome in the little gray cottage, it is because of the hospitality I found in waiting for every stranger in the quaint old Square,—in the Bishop's home, in the Sister's House, in the church and in the school,—that I have wished to record one stranger's impression of a Salem Easter, and of the Moravian faith.

I wish that I might have been present for all the church services of this reverent preparation week, for Palm Sunday and the confirmation, for Maundy Thursday and the evening communion commemorative of the first sacramental supper. Day by day, through all the week, the congregation has heard read, the "Acts of Monday," the "Acts of Tuesday," and so on, the services consisting of the reading of

17

the gospel record constantly interspersed
with the rich singing of the old chorales.
I wish I had been here in Salem through
all these days that have approached nearer
and nearer to Easter in reverent proces-
sional.   The afternoon service of Good
Friday is my first introduction to the
Moravian liturgy.   I am familiar with the
ceremonial of palled altar and penitential
abasement and despair, but this Moravian
Good Friday is without a hint of gloom.
Grown-ups   and   bright-faced   children
crowd the church, all quiet yet with a stir
of cheery friendliness.   The organ rolls
solemn yet not sad.   The choir files in
simply, and quite as simply the Bishop, in
ordinary dress, takes his seat below them
close to his people as if he were but one of
them.   My first impression of the Moravian service is of informality combined
with profound, spontaneous reverence,
and the second is its deep, pervasive joy-
ousness.   Is it this last that has kept burning so clear the lamp of the spirit in the
Bishop's eyes in spite of his eighty years?
The   faces   of   God's   stewards   grow
strangely alike as their frail crafts draw
near the harbour beacons.   The bishop's

face, with the Easter light upon it, as his familiar figure moves about these old streets, will always for me embody all Salem's Easter welcome to the stranger.

As the Bishop reads that old, cruel record of the lots cast for the seamless robe, and of the brutal spear, I perceive the strong triumph by which the light of Easter makes radiant even the blackness of the crucifixion. Through all the service, music is the chief element, for the Moravian custom makes the whole-hearted hymn-singing of the entire congregation the very well-spring of worship; a faith whose central theme is Easter expresses itself in a liturgy which consists more of praise than of prayer. Even through the slow roll of the Good Friday hymns there seems to run as undercurrent the strong pæan of the coming resurrection, so that the image before one's vision is not so much the torturing cruelty of the cross as the beauty of a willing sacrifice. The singing of selected stanzas of familiar hymns is as spontaneous as the informal Sunday night singing of some family group, and it is as if the Bishop's prayer were uttered by one member of a great family fellowship, "Into thy widespread arms, stretched out upon the cross, receive us all. Amen."

We pour out from the old hooded doorway down the many-trodden stone steps into the flooding westward sunshine. Many people go toward the graveyard as if for a brief passing greeting to those gentle sunny mounds. A backward glance at the old church shows the weather-vane arrow and glittering ball and the steadfast clock-face beneath, all ashine. For more than a hundred years they have never failed to give back the unfailing sunset. From that white belfry is always sounded the death announcement made triumphant in sonorous music. Either at noon or at fall of evening the trombones will peal forth those old familiar tunes informing the listeners whether it was child or grown-up, man or woman, married or single, that soul for whom, from high in air, the ancient horns blow a bon voyage on its passage skyward.

The mood of the afternoon service holds the mind until the evening love-feast. We use the word love-feast so

often flippantly that I did not dream
how instantly its deep significance would
impress me. I begin to feel the spirit
before we go to the church, in the hospitality with which Miss Bertha gathers
five of us to accompany her so that we
may not fancy ourselves tonight to be
strangers in the old Home Church. She
gives each of us a little napkin in which
we are to cover up the love-feast bun
when we first receive it. The fragrance
of coffee meets us as we enter. The organ
rolls forth, slow and solemn beneath a
master touch. Throughout the congregation there runs a low rustle of cordiality.
It is impossible to explain, it is only possible to experience, the profound effect
upon the emotions of the strange ming-
ling of informality and of deep religious
dignity. The essential idea of the love-
feast is to symbolize the brotherhood of
man with man, our welded fellowship,
since it was for every one of us alike that
God suffered in human flesh, died, and
was buried.

The measured sorrow of the organ suddenly peals in triumph. The choir files
in, and then the Bishop and the Pastor

take their places near us behind a snowy table. They are in ordinary dress and seat themselves side by side facing the congregation. The Pastor rises and briefly reviews the events of Passion week as one by one the services have commemorated them. At last the anguish is finished, he tells us, and tonight, we are gathered in a quiet garden before a sealed tomb. He reads the account of the burial, and in the bright-lit church, among whose worshippers are many, many children, their happy wondering faces subdued by that solemn evening narrative so simply read, we all see the reverent tending of a swathed body by Joseph of Arimathæa and Nicodemus. We watch the great rock sealed and hear the clink of metal trappings as the Roman sentinels take up their watch beneath white stars.

The Pastor's prayer is brief. He prays that we may remember that without the sacrifice of Christ now consummated within the sealed tomb there would never have been the beauty of Christian fellowship as tonight we experience it. Then a hymn rings out,

" Lamb of God, thy precious blood,
Healing wounds and bitter death,
Be our trust, our only boast.
Blessed object of our faith,
Thy once marrèd countenance
Comfort to our hearts dispense;
By thy anguish, stripes and pain,
May we life and strength obtain."

At the close of that stanza the choir
begins an anthem, and as it sounds, a door
at the side opens and through it, with a
reverent decorum that somehow catches at
the heart-strings, there moves in a file of
eight white-clad women, some of them
girls, some of them silver-headed. They
carry great baskets of love-feast buns.
The head "diener" serves first the Bishop
and Pastor, and then the buns are dis-
tributed throughout the congregation, so
quietly, so reverently that one scarcely
hears a rustle of movement throughout
the entire church. Noiselessly the white
procession passes back through the door it
had entered, and now comes a line of men
carrying trays loaded with straight white
mugs of coffee. Just as the buns, so the
mugs, are given to each person present.
The bun we have folded in our napkin,

the mug we hold, for the moment has not arrived for tasting. The whole building is ringing with Watts' deathless stanza,

> " When I survey the wondrous cross,
>   On which the Prince of Glory died,
> My richest gain I count but loss,
>   And pour contempt on all my pride."

Then the congregation yields place to the choir, and while a soprano voice soars sweet, telling of that green hill far away, the love-feast is eaten. There follows more singing by the people while the elders re-enter and collect the empty cups, to the accompaniment of the words:

> " Let us for each other care,
>   Each his brother's burden bear,
> To thy church a pattern give,
>   Showing how believers live."

The Bishop rises to make the Good Friday address, but his words are not of death and burial, they are of life and of heaven. To the creed which the Bishop inherits, Good Friday is but a transient gloom across the golden triumph of Easter. The Bishop is eighty, he stands near enough to catch sometimes the

strains they sing who have reached
harbour. How many home-goings he
must have heard sounded by the trombones from the white belfry! That is why
his words dwell so gladly upon our recog-
nitions beyond the grave. Not only shall
we greet relatives and friends long gone,
but we shall look about us and recognise
others: the sad and suffering whom at
some time we have comforted; the strong
and good who at some time have comforted us, and with these, still others,
those true comrades who have joined
hands with us in helping. We shall experience a rapt new life of fellowship,
marvellous now to gaze upon. Yet our
present duty is not to contemplate but to
prepare, and the best way to prepare for
the fellowship to come is by cementing
fellowship each with our neighbour here,
yet never forgetting our nearness even
now on earth to our loved ones beyond.
We cannot guess, the Bishop says, how
near even at this instant heaven may be.
Its farthest reaches may lie unimaginably
distant but its lowest step may touch our
hands, if we but stretch them out. With
a sudden flash of inspiration he drives

home the love-feast truth. "At this very
instant," so he begs each one of us, "pray
for the person sitting to your left, the person sitting to your right, that together
with you, all three may receive, together,
God's peculiar blessing needed for each
life." By such prayer each for his neighbour, shall the current of love-feast blessing flow strong and unbroken, uniting
perhaps with the stream of affection
flooding toward us from those passed on
who love us still, for what earth-bound
brain can fathom,—so the Bishop's rapt
voice questions—the full meaning of those
familiar words, the communion of saints,
which tonight we have gathered to symbolize in solemn Easter love-feast.

Strangely near they seemed to me, near
as eyes alight with deathless love, those
stars that burned white and clear above
us, as with the Bishop's words still throb-
bing in our ears, we poured forth, on that
Good Friday evening, into the quiet
Square. Stars and sun were both the
lights of Easter on that long-ago Pass-
over, stars that kept watch above a grave
"wherein was never man yet laid," sun
that saw the victory over the grave that

never before had man conquered. Over
God's acre beyond my bedroom window
on that Good Friday night, the Easter
stars burned steadfast.

III

THE SALEM OF THE PAST

IT is a sun-flooded Saturday, that of the "Great Sabbath," and astir with preparations. All day long the graveyard is a place of pilgrimage, as I look down from my window at its sunny reaches. The "graveyard" is sharply different from the modern "cemetery"; always in Salem the distinction in names is kept. The "cemetery" is just beyond the slope and appears curiously alien with its many-shaped monuments and vaults and sarcophagi all irregularly grouped, all insistently individual. Tranquil by contrast are the long lines of little rectangular slabs lying side by side on the Moravian graves. The stones on the first green mounds are gray and old, the last are white and fresh, but today, on Great Sabbath, they will all be scoured clean by loving hands, so that the simple epitaphs will show clear with their dates, from 1771 to the present, and with their recorded birthplaces of the long ago dead, Saxony, Denmark, Sweden, Holland, England. All day there is happy activity in those carefully tended green spaces. In the bright morning a sprite of four passes our gate, and we call out to her, "What are you going to do?"

She swings a little tin pail gaily as she answers, "Going to scrub graves."

All day long that busy, happy scouring is continued. There are no flowers planted on any of the graves, but everywhere cut flowers and flower-pieces are being heaped on the grassy mounds. Few of the oldest graves have many blossoms, but at the top of every stone is laid a bunch of ivy leaves. No one of all the sleepers is forgotten by the living.

Three visits that I make today emphasize the constant effort of all Moravians to keep alive the spirit and the spirits of their past. There is no barren extolling of dead days, but, rather, a blending of them with the present, a conscious, vital union with the traditions and the purposes of founders whose wise foresight has been amply proved. In old Salem, tradition continues as recurrent and as freshly green as the grass upon the Easter graves. The dead live, that is the fundamental of the Moravian creed, a truth held so absolutely that it ramifies from dogma into every department of daily life, and accounts for the meticulous care with which the records of church and community and family have been kept. The little archive house of Salem is a mine of delight for the student of history. The lady who unlocks its door for me, and unlocks also the secrets of the busy human drama still alive within those old German documents, traces her ancestry back to more than one name famous in the annals of the Moravian church and in the founding of Salem. For her the hours spent with those yellowing parchments are full of a discoverer's ardour. From one shelf and another she takes down now a parish register, or history, now some legal deed, or some private diary, and opening to me that neat German script, she makes alive for me long-dead men and women,—their industry, their pioneer pluck, their consecrated common sense. There in the low rooms of the archive house certain indi-

IN THE DEEP FIREPLACE THE COFFEE IS STILL BOILED FOR THE LOVE FEASTS OF THE PRESENT

viduals flash forth: young Count Zinzendorf, whose burning zeal made his life from babyhood to death a romance of religion, so practical a mystic, so adventurous a saint, so high-hearted a victim when persecuted; Christian David, that daring carpenter, who engineered so many little bands out from cruel Bohemia to Zinzendorf's city of refuge, Herrnhut, —one sees Christian David, as he fells the first tree of that settlement in Saxony, swinging his axe and quoting, "The sparrow hath found an house, and the swallow a nest for herself, where she may lay her young, even thine altars, O Lord of hosts." A stout axe, an intrepid trust, a constant searching of Scripture, these seem to have been the unvarying equipment of all Moravian pioneers, both the famous and the humble, both in Zinzendorf's Saxony, and here in their Wachovian grant in North Carolina. Looking down from a wall in the archive house is the keen and genial face of Bishop Spangenberg, whom his friend Zinzendorf nick-named "Joseph" because he was so kind to his brethren. It was in 1752 that Bishop Spangenberg was deputed by

Zinzendorf to select the 100,000 acres
that should comprise the Moravian tract
purchased from Lord Granville in North
Carolina. It cost Bishop Spangenberg
and his companions a dozen weeks of
hardship and exploration in an unknown
wilderness before they discovered a region
suited to their purpose; because it re-
minded them of the fertile meadows of
their Saxon home, they named it Wachau,
Wachovia.

Some months after the region had been
thus selected and surveyed, its first colonists set forth. Careful records made by
that first band of Moravian settlers tell us
how they started out from Bethlehem,
Pennsylvania, on October 8, 1753, twelve
"Single Brethren" carefully selected to
be conquerors of the wilderness as well as
founders of a religious colony,—pastor,
farmers, carpenters, a baker, a doctor
whose ministry was to spread over a
radius of a hundred miles. On Saturday
evening, November 17th, the little procession,—men, horses, and one covered
wagon—reached the empty cabin which
was to be their wilderness shelter. There
on that first Saturday night while, as their

own chroniclers tell us, the wolves and panthers howled outside the door, they held their first love-feast. From those first years down to today the chief historians have been the pastors. At present the custom is still most carefully kept of reading the "Memorabilia" of the events of the past year at the watch-night services held on New Year's Eve. Just as in 1753 Pastor Grube kept the records of his parish and read them aloud to his people at New Year's, so today Bishop Rondthaler reads his "Memorabilia" to his congregation in the last hours of every year. While the "Memorabilia" are chiefly concerned with events happening in Salem, they have also, both in the eighteenth century and now, always contained references to events occurring in the state and the nation and in the world at large. This custom has brought it about that sometimes the records of some obscure Moravian parish have settled the date of some historic incident of national significance.

I could have lingered long among those carefully labelled chronicles enshrining so many long-gone human personalities, and cherished with the same perception of the value of sequence as is shown by the tending of the old hallowed graves. Salem is a city that never forgets what it owes to its founders, and so in humble human imitation of a divine Easter gesture, rolls away the stone of oblivion that would restrain their resurgent influence. It is a little later in this day and at the scene of their first efforts that those sturdy old builders of the old Wachovian colony come forth from the past to my vision, all quick with life and energy.

It is a ten miles drive from Salem, not founded until 1766, to Bethabara, or "Old Town," the first village of Wachovia. Here the early colonists built the sturdy little church, which stands today, unchanged inside or out, as it was when consecrated in 1769. Church and parsonage form one building; the parsonage is now a parish house containing the love-feast kitchen; in the deep fireplace the coffee is still boiled for the love-feasts of the present, and in the big cupboards the straight white mugs are stacked. Grouped about the church are old houses, their stucco walls a mellow buff against which are massed great green domes of boxwood.

THE DEAD LIVE; THAT IS THE FUNDAMENTAL OF THE MORAVIAN CREED

At the back of the church begins the line
of stone posts lately erected to mark the
stockade which protected the settlement
during the Indian wars. The Moravian
villages were originally on friendly terms
with their Indian neighbours, but as the
spirit of treachery and murder spread
South from the Northern tribes to infect
the Cherokees, the pioneers were forced to
build their stockade and to load their
guns. Many scattered settlers fled to
their protection, and the administration
of a crowded refugee community was a
difficult task. There was much sickness
and many a stealthy burial party had to
climb to the hill-top graveyard in the
night lest the Indians discover how few
and weak were the defenders of the fort

That hill-top burial-ground of Old
Town, no one who has ever visited it could
ever forget. It is the highest point of all
the country round, so lofty that its trees
served as watch-towers against Indian
attack. The great chestnuts and oaks of
1750 still stand sentinel over the little flat
gray stones, hidden deep in grass and blue
periwinkle. It was in some immemorial
April that those trees first thrust forth

the pale shoots that once again today veil
the gaunt, sinewy boughs. Towering and
undecayed the great trees still sway and
whisper on their high and wind-rocked
hill. At the foot of one great trunk is a
tiny grave, tender in the memory, like the
blue of periwinkle. It is the oldest grave
in Wachovia, and yet the grave of so
young a little spirit! The date on the
stone is 1757, and the name of the two-
year-old is Anna Maria Opiz. I wonder
if in the other world there is periwinkle,
blossoming eternally fresh and blue. It
was from a heart strong in deathless
Easter hope that the old diarist wrote of
the baby girl, "She was gathered in as the
first floweret in Wachovia by our Heav-
enly Gardener and her little tenement was
sown as the first grain of wheat in this
God's acre, which upon this occasion was
consecrated."

Moravian creed and custom have always had a peculiar reverence for child-
hood. The boys and girls of today seem
to grow up into the faith of their fathers
as happily and loyally as spring blossoms
develop into fruitage. In methods of
education there must always have been an

THE BEAUTIFUL GROUNDS OF SALEM ACADEMY
ARE HIDDEN BEHIND THE BUILDINGS THAT
FLANK THE SQUARE

exercise of that gracious tact in tending little budding souls which is first recorded as a rule for Christian practice in the tenth chapter of Mark. Bethlehem and Salem have each had for more than a hundred years a famous school for girls. In many a Southern family of today, grandmother, mother, and daughter have all attended Salem Academy, and still in an unbroken tradition Salem Academy and Salem College will receive the daughters of tomorrow. As their grandmothers have done they will sit on late spring afternoons on the steps beneath the white pillars, or in the grounds hidden behind those high brick buildings that flank the Square, they will wander beneath the dreaming willows and linger by the little tinkling fountains.

At the southern end of the brick façade, but forming one continuous line with the newer buildings, is the old Sisters' House; here lives one whose life has formed an unbroken line of continuity between the old time and the new. For fifty years Miss L. was a teacher, watching the Academy grow from the standards of a grade school to those of a college, and far

more than that, herself leading, directing,
establishing those growing standards. As
a graduate of those earlier elementary
courses, she blazed her own trail into
fuller knowledge, always keeping ahead
of her classes and leading them after her.
Frail, alert, alive, an eager flame lightly
cased in the fragile seventies, I shall not
soon forget the delicate, slim figure, or the
mobile face beneath the short white curls.

The Sisters' House was for me a
place of subtle, speculative memories,—
this home of the "single sisters," a group
of women who gave their lives to service,
and were, during a period when in most
places "old maid" was a term of op-
probrium, here regarded with veneration
as an integral part of the community. It
seems to me that from every aspect from
which I, a stranger, could observe it, the
Moravian practice has succeeded in nour-
ishing tradition in such a way as to make
it still bear the old sound mellow fruit
under new and modern conditions. The
old Sisters' House with its bare white-
washed walls, its broad-planked floors, its
quaint cul-de-sac corridors, has adapted
itself so far as possible to the independ-

ence of a modern apartment building. In rooms big enough to be arranged for all the requirements of a tiny modern flat the retired teachers now spend their old age. To the last they are a live influence. Former pupils are constantly dropping in at the Sisters' House, and the students of today know their way through those netted old corridors. In the big dining-room hundreds of girls bow their heads when Miss L., a slender figure leaning on a slender cane, stands to ask the blessing. Both in their homes and in their schools the Moravians have found the secret of an education that unites the aged and the youthful as naturally as bough and blossom are united. In most educational systems there is no servitor more quickly condemned to the scrap-heap than the old teacher, but the Moravians have too deep an insight into values to practice so blind and heartless an economy. I wonder if the girls today going forth from Salem College will carry through life any deeper educative influence than that of Miss L.'s presence in an old room of many welcomes, a room still cordially open to anyone's knock.

IV

A SALEM EASTER

THESE three visits on this "Great Sabbath," to the archive house where the dead founders are still valiantly alive, to the Sisters' House where past and present are one, to the Bethabara graveyard where the trees of two centuries are once more green with youth, these three visits have put my spirit in tune for the Easter vigil. That vigil is ushered in by the gathering twilight, in which we sit with Miss Dorcas on her porch, watching the few late visitors still busy in the graveyard. Laden down with wreaths and bouquets, which she has spent all afternoon in arranging, Miss Bertha has gone to "my graves," as Miss Dorcas calls them. One friend after another drops in to chat awhile with us seated there on the dusky porch, while the gold of the sunset fades gently to gray, and the stars steal forth. There are chil-

dren bobbing about, laughing, rolling on
the green stretches in the happy evening,
all talking of the mysterious antics of the
Easter rabbit expected to make his rounds
tomorrow morning. Miss Dorcas speaks
in tranquil comment, "You think so much
about the dead today, don't you? I am
getting so old I shall be going any
time now." Her words chime with the
Bishop's who when someone asked him
who was to conduct the Easter services,
answered smiling, "I *say* that I shall, but
when a man is eighty, he cannot know."
True Moravians who have seen so many
glad Easters cannot face death with any
shudder, for they know their going will
be told in music on the evening wind, that
their graves on every Easter will be
jocund with flowers, that their memories
will be kept radiant in the fellowship of
the living with the dead.

A young nephew of my friend's, blow-
ing in upon her for a breezy greeting,
says, "So near the graveyard? Aren't
you afraid of ghosts?" then adds, "But I
never heard of a Moravian ghost." If
they could come back, Moravian ghosts,
they would be sweet, dim visitants whom

no one could fear,—that is my thought as I look out on their quiet sleeping place just before I get into bed.

Full of preparations, Miss Bertha has bustled us off to sleep early, but before we go upstairs she has made Miss Dorcas comfortable for the night, and has also arranged the couch for the little neighbour, Margaret Anne, who is to stay here tonight in order to go with us to the early service. Both fall asleep all eager expectancy, eight years old and eighty, side by side.

Miss Bertha is briskly winding her alarm clock when we say goodnight. She assures us that she will call us in good time for coffee and sugar cake with her at five.

Our sleep is fitful. Old Salem does not expect to sleep much on Easter Even. All night, steps crunch the gravel outside our windows. All night motor cars pour into the old streets from all the country round. Dreamily the noises drift in to me and now and then I start up for a brief wakeful moment at the chiming of the church clock. It is half past one when my friend's eager whisper rouses me, makes me hurry to kneel beside her at the dark window, for we must not miss the gathering of the trombone bands who shall go forth through all the sleeping streets announcing Easter. In the deep sky the Easter stars are shining, white above the dim squares in the long lines in the graveyard. One great window glows forth in the surrounding dark, the window of the room in the old Beloe House where they have been giving the band members coffee before their march. Just below us near the church, a mellow voice is speaking directions. There is moving to and fro of shadowy forms assembling. Through the gloom bob the ruddy orbs of torches, the night is too still for any flaring streamers of light. The shapes of men and boys are indistinct, but the torch glow shines clear on the metal of the long horns. Every Moravian boy knows how to play the trombone. There are fathers and sons and uncles in the groups mustering now. Boys too small to sound a horn may carry a torch. They are all gathering quietly, reverently. The voice of the director sounds low and clear through the Square, as one by one he dismisses a band of a score on its appointed march. Each band will have its particular tunes, its particular places for playing them. At exactly the same corner beneath our window Miss Dorcas has for forty years heard the same tune played. The cherished stanza to which her memory fits those measures she has had Miss Bertha write down for us. As two o'clock chimes from the dim belfry in the dark sky the trombones ring out on the stillness. Somewhere down in the silent house below us, Miss Dorcas is listening, whispering the words for which the music is the accompaniment:

> " Thy majesty, how vast it is,
>   And how immense the glory,
> Which thou, O Jesus, dost possess,
>   Both heaven and earth adore thee;
> The legions of angels exult thy great name,
>   Thy glory and might are transcendent,
> And thousands and thousands thy praises
>   proclaim,
>   Upon thee gladly dependent."

For some minutes we hear the measured beat of their steps as band after band goes out from the old Square. For two hours, sounding now here, now there, distant yet poignant and clear, the ancient horns will peal forth their message. From our window we watch one company march down Cedar Avenue. Beyond that quiet avenue, we can hear the clang and rush of trolleys, the barking of automobiles. We watch the gleaming torches and dim-lit brass as the company tramps past the ivied gate posts and the arches with their texts of hope, while, white in the dusk and the stars, the long ranks of the flowered gravestones keep their measured march step by step accompanying the living. The torches bob to the rise and fall of those rhythmic feet, successors of feet that once, mad with unearthly joy, sped through dark streets, to tell men grief-bowed in black Jerusalem, of a golden morning.

The sweet Easter music rings at intervals through the few hours of sleep left. It does not seem long before we hear Miss Bertha stirring about, and presently we are on our way downstairs. The windows are still coal-black squares and we eat by electric light. The table is gay with red tulips. Margaret Anne bows her little square-cropped head to ask the old Moravian blessing,

" Come, Lord Jesus, our guest to be
And bless the gifts bestowed by thee."

The coffee and sugar cake are delicious,
and, by Miss Dorcas's special request,
there is also a plate of delicate white cook-
ies, "white Christmas cakes." There are
also in the holiday season, as Miss Bertha
tells us, "black Christmas cakes." The
conversation passes easily to Salem
Christmas customs. I should like to be
present at the children's Christmas Eve
festival when the old church is all in dark-
ness except for the lighted tapers, given
to each child. A Saviour born to brighten
this dark earth, a Saviour coming forth
bright from a dark tomb,—as I look into
Margaret Anne's glowing Easter face, I
perceive that here in Moravian Salem the
story of a birth and the story of a resurrection are blent into a creed simple
enough for any child to understand.

It is still dark at half-past five when we
go out into the street. As Miss Anna's
guests we have the good fortune to be ad-
mitted within the ropes which bar all entrance to the Square and also cut off the
streets leading up to the graveyard. Be-

yond the Square, from earliest morning
there has been gathering a phalanxed
crowd stretching for blocks. We wait
close to the church among the members
of the home congregation. Just across
from us is the side wall and sloping roof-
gable of an old brick house. Against this
house wall in the dusk and shadow the
trombone bands, returned two hours ago,
are massed. Their torches glow orbed
and ruddy, gleaming now on the polished
shaft of a long horn, now on some face
suddenly flashing forth against the dark.
Above the house roof there is lacework of
woven branches softened by their first
leaf-shoots. Beyond the branches floats
the silver wafer of the Pascal moon, shining through ravelled cloud.

We wait there with eyes glued to the
hooded front of the old church door.
"Watch!" whispers Miss Bertha, for we
must not miss the opening of that door.
At last an electric light flashes up within
the arched entrance. No word is spoken
anywhere. The doors swing in. First
come the ushers, then the choir, next the
pastors of all the Moravian churches of
the city, and then the mayor. Still we

wait, watching the door. It is as if all the congregation in the Square and all those close-packed thousands in the surrounding streets,—it is as if each of us drew a long breath, waiting. Suddenly, silently, he is there, an old man standing in the stream of light from the church entrance. For blocks and blocks of dark streets people will hear his voice, a beautiful voice now pushed to its uttermost,— "The Lord is risen! He is risen indeed!"

Unnoticed the whiteness of morning has become visible against the outlines of old roofs. The tension of expectancy slackens into the beauty of realization. As with one single spontaneous voice the old Square sings:

> " Hail, all hail, victorious Lord and Saviour,
>   Thou hast burst the bonds of death;
>   Grant, as to Mary, the great favour
>   To embrace thy feet in faith:
>   Thou hast in our stead the curse endured,
>   And for us eternal life procured;
>   Joyful we with one accord,
>   Hail thee as our risen Lord."

The Easter liturgy is the affirmation of triumphant belief. One by one the

Bishop reads first the statement of faith in the Father, and at the close the congregation proclaims assent,

"This I verily believe."

Then in low reverent murmur the Lord's prayer rises. Next the Bishop reads, sentence after sentence, the articles that embody the faith in God's Son, to which the congregation responds,

"This I most certainly believe."

The Bishop's voice rings last in the words of belief in the Holy Ghost, and a third time the congregation affirms its creed,

"This I assuredly believe."

The stanza of a hymn closes the service in the Square, which is now broken by the march to the graveyard, where the "Easter Morning Litany" will be completed. The Bishop now addresses "those of many faiths, from many places gathered here." He begs those far crowds, in the name of the risen Lord, to move quietly, each person mindful of each other's need, each preserving the Easter spirit, as all march, forming into fours, congregation and visitors all proceeding in long unbroken column to the graveyard. The Bishop leads the procession. He wears a black cap, a long black overcoat, which, buttoned to the throat, faintly suggests the outline of a black gown, but there is absolutely no insignia, no hint of ceremonial. The Bishop is but one of a great concourse whom he leads to celebrate the Resurrection.

The first trombone band follows just behind the Bishop. The others come at intervals. They play antiphonally, passing their music back along the line as runners might pass a torch. Day is brightening everywhere. The moon has become a dead gray wisp. The dim scene grows palpitant with colour, the bright emerald of poplars, the soft red of old brick, the dense green of boxwood, the black-green of ivy, and against an old buff wall the drooping lavendar grace of wistaria. The procession passes along the wide gravel path of Cedar Avenue between the lines of poplars. The gray stone wall that, on our left, separates Cedar Avenue from the town, is alive with watching faces. A father balances a wondering baby on that low parapet. The head of a bright-turbanned black

mammy shows at another point. Every
twelve feet along the march there is sta-
tioned an usher, wearing a tiny bit of red
and white ribbon in his lapel. There
are a hundred and fifty of these ushers.
They stand with bared heads and reverent faces. The great crowd obeys the
slightest motion of an usher's hand. The
simple, grave decorum is dominant everywhere. The Bishop enters at the middle
gate, passing beneath the white arch in-
scribed, "I am the Resurrection and the
Life." He takes his stand at the center
of the graveyard. The crowd is massed
solidly in the broad intersecting paths.
There are no ropes to protect the graves,
but yet not a foot transgresses on their
privacy. At every entrance now the
crowd flows in, in steady fours endlessly.
As he passes beneath the lettered arches,
every man bares his head. Within the
graveyard all face toward the Bishop. In
the long reverent waiting for all to as-
semble, there is a low hum of talk but no
noise anywhere. The birds, jocund at
seven of a radiant March morning, can be
clearly heard in the budding branches over
our heads. The service is always timed to

take place exactly at sunrise, but today it
has been impossible to calculate the length
of time it will take the procession to enter.
The sun shows first a burning rim, then
climbs to balance a scarlet disk on the far
horizon beyond the trees, and is mounting
high above the hill line, while still the
crowd streams into the graveyard, twenty
thousand when they have finished.

As we wait, the air is sweet with the
flowers upon the graves. I wonder if we
stand there alone, we who call ourselves
"the living." Perhaps there bend to us
above the white stones gracious presences
from long ago. Who shall fathom at any
time the subtle interweaving of life with
death? Here in the sunny graveyard
little gray crumbled slabs bear the blithe
names mothers once sang in the lullabies
of long-dead babies. Today blithe,
bubbly, living children crowd close upon
the lichened stones. Margaret Anne's
hand is warm in mine. This is her first
sunrise service. When she goes home she
will hunt for the gifts the Easter rabbit
will have left for her.

Still we watch the in-pouring of that
great crowd, until in the distance we hear

the notes of the trombone band at the end
of the procession, and at last all are gathered within the ivied portals, and there
among the flower-heaped graves the beautiful Easter litany is completed. The old
hymns float up above the branches. Far
over the hushed concourse the Bishop's
voice rings in the age-old words of deathless triumph:

"I have a desire to depart, and to be
with Christ, which is far better: I shall
never taste death; yea, I shall attain unto
the resurrection of the dead: for the body
which I shall put off, this grain of cor-
ruptibility, shall put on incorruption; my
flesh shall rest in hope.

"And the God of peace that brought
again from the dead our Lord Jesus, the
great Shepherd of the sheep, through the
blood of the everlasting covenant, shall
also quicken these our mortal bodies if so
be that the Spirit of God hath dwelt in
them."

In deep murmured unison sounds the
response, "We poor sinners pray, hear us,
gracious Lord and God."

Then come words that express the in-
most spirit of this graveyard service,

words that embody the aspiration that has made Easter the key of the Moravian creed:

"And keep us in everlasting fellowship with those of our brethren and sisters who, since last Easter-day, have entered into the joy of their Lord, and with the whole church triumphant, and let us rest together in thy presence from our labours."

When the service is completed, the great crowd in silence pours forth again through the white-arched entrances, thridding the streets of the city in all directions, moving homeward. One cannot talk, going home from that Easter worship by the graves.

Even when, in the afternoon, we leave old Salem, we cannot talk much, for the peace of a beautiful memory holds our spirits too deeply for any words. The crowding, whizzing cars, returning, make the highway a blur of noise and dust, a highway leading away from Easter into the busy hum of every day. Days and weeks and months shall turn their swift wheels bearing me far from Salem. Yet always that word will have power to release memories as fragrant as flowers placed tenderly within the hands of happy sleepers, a memory of a baby girl cradled beneath a great tree on a windy hill top, a memory of an old man's voice, invincible in faith, that rings through dim streets upon an Easter dawn:

"The Lord is risen! He is risen indeed!"

Printed in United States of America.